RIOT LUNG

RIOT LUNG

LEAH HORLICK

*To amanda,
with all of the
full moon and valentine's
wishes! xox*

thistledown press

Thistledown Press Ltd.
118 - 20th Street West
Saskatoon, Saskatchewan, S7M 0W6
www.thistledownpress.com

Library and Archives Canada Cataloguing in Publication

Horlick, Leah
Riot lung / Leah Horlick.

Poems.
ISBN 978-1-927068-08-3

I. Title.

PS8615.O745R56 2012   C811'.6   C2012-904722-8

Cover and book design by Jackie Forrie
Printed and bound in Canada

Thistledown Press gratefully acknowledges the financial assistance of the Canada Council
for the Arts, the Saskatchewan Arts Board, and the Government of Canada through the
Canada Book Fund for its publishing program.

ACKNOWLEDGEMENTS

All gratitude to my parents, Anna Power and Allan Horlick, my brother Nicholas, and my grandparents Sylvia & Doug Power and Ruth & Louis Horlick, whose unconditional support is a blessing. Gratitude also to our dear family friends Elizabeth Brewster, Martha Blum, and Anne Szumigalski for their earliest words of encouragement.

Poems in Riot Lung originally appeared in *Grain* and *So To Speak*. My appreciation to the editors of each. The italicized lines in "Yartzeit" are used with humble gratitude and are selected from, in order of appearance: Langston Hughes, "Poem"; Judy Grahn, "A Woman is Talking to Death"; Allen Ginsberg, "Howl". The epigraph in "saskatoon psalm" is from e.e. cummings' *Collected Poems 1962-1964*.

wreckoning was originally published as a limited-edition, handmade chapbook in collaboration with Alison Roth Cooley. My thanks to Alison, JackPine Collective, Elise Marcella Godfrey, and Anne Simpson for all their dedication.

Thank you to editor Susan Musgrave and the team at Thistledown Press for their invaluable guidance, support, and feedback.

This book was a joy to write because of the Tonight It's Poetry Collective and reading series. Particular gratitude to Taylor Leedahl, Stephen Rutherford, Lisa Johnson, Charles Hamilton, and Nicole Almond.

To Calondra Mainhart, the first to see all my first drafts, and Adrienne Gruber, for the gift of her mentorship and friendship from coast to coast.

This book was written with love for and fondest memories of Braedon Carignan (1988-2010). My gratitude to his family and our friends for their support and grace.

These poems were written, performed, and edited on Treaty Six Cree and unceded Coast Salish territories.

for Brady

CONTENTS

I can tell you this much about the light

In April we head up to St. Louis to see the ghost light
leaving the city and its cichlid pools of neon,
its dust storms and concrete bracken
for a highway empty and spring-withered.

If you're looking, dim your brights at the drive-in
pass the railroad crossing with red lights shuttered,
fluorescent cross fixed on a dark hill —

the hotel swamped in gravel, Coke sign
jaundiced, and the bridge as shadowy
as I remember.

Park in the ditch. Check for company
at the boxcar sunk ahead in the snow:
only the dead skunk, a black cat —
peripheral trick-shapes.

Leave a trail of camera flash.
Wait for ghosts, grins of spectral
teeth.

I can tell you this much about the light
it comes and goes like sapient wind,
quicksilver in syllables, white radial pulses
at the end of the dirt road.

They say it's all that's left of the engine
that ran the tracks out here.

They say a lot of things as the light washes
in and out, ghosts of trains we never caught.

Welcome to all tourists and sportsmen

Spring migration: we drive into town past the alpaca farm
and bison ranch. Mom thinks I'm asleep in the back seat.
Whispers to my dad *where the fuck are you taking me.*

My mother, maritimer, will shoot the next neighbour
who, for housewarming, tells her *a waving wheat field
is like the ocean* —except we're the family without guns.

Open season: my mother takes me and my baby brother
to the laundromat to keep the hunters' orange overalls
and muddy boots away.

The woman at the co-op yells at her across the street
hey lady, is that all you ever wear is black?

No place for hibernation: we pull up our spindling roots
with the train tracks.

Leave town in the wake of the one-block fire,
elevator skeleton, gas station robbed dry.

In black sweaters pitch and roll on the highway,
dry heaves of wheat behind us.

red earth

coldest night,
when the reserve girls hit the rink

tall on their skates, braids pulled back,
mouth-guarded jaws

we hid in the walls like field mice,
felt them slam into boards and rattle

cracked our knuckles, plowed hockey stops
into sawdust, chewed our nails.

after the game, your parents cut
your hair short again.

we walk into snow packing
chins up, swagger of blades
on our feet.

no more

you and i, we lock ourselves in the empty room
at your parents' motel, hide

call your fake boyfriend collect
in wisconsin, sing

in breathy voices. he wants us to meet him
at the mall. *what mall?*

we are twelve. the cold sore in the corner
of your mouth is crusted in sugar.

we want candy necklaces, to swap
lip gloss, no one knows

which of us is the bad influence
you, noisy trouble in platforms

sneaking me girl magazines
from the truck stop, running

across the highway at night
for pop rocks and snickers

until my mother says no more —
or is it me, stealing kittens from ditches

for our familiars until your mother
says *no more* —

no more running, no more night
highways, witchcraft

nothing can protect us here, not
anymore, not even magic.

let me tell you about where i come from

a place maybe like yours: somewhere
the highway goes through for a reason

downwind of weyerhaeuser, rural municipality
of rumours and racism, a place

where a cree girl couldn't buy lysol
if her clean floors depended on it

a town that taught me never to wear lipstick
and hitchhike

the shoulder of the number twenty-three
where ears flattened i could hear a truck
miles away shifting eighteen gears to stop,
rattling gravel

i lost all my high school sweethearts
to meth, fort mac, and the tar sands.

the girl I ran my lemonade stand with
hanged herself

my best friends became
cougar, coyote, and jailbait

our favourite games were always chicken:

spread-eagled on the asphalt, how long
before someone runs us over

thumbs out, how long
before someone picks us up

a place where the answer
is never long enough.

shelterbelt

ok now you be the gravel shoulder
ditch's slope of shadows & startled eyes
dark fringe of treeline, shelterbelt & wet slough roots
you square up to the sky this time and against
the scarlet fever where the city grows, fill
the empty elevator space in my skyline.

saskatchewan sex ed

a man in a bar once told me
foreplay is when you pull her hair first
and if it don't fall out, she don't got aids.

⊲⊷⊳ ⊲⊷⊳ ⊲⊷⊳

it's a waterfall and second base is
drowning.

⊲⊷⊳ ⊲⊷⊳ ⊲⊷⊳

seventh grade, first communion
and born-again virgin
certificate.

⊲⊷⊳ ⊲⊷⊳ ⊲⊷⊳

they taught me
to put a condom
on a full-grown
banana.

Itchy Legs

Here, the welts from the two-hour river walk
wading in sweetgrass up to my knees:

new tattoos swollen with red from mosquitoes
who teethed on my ankles last night

the blue stripe of a bruise where I drove,
a tank full of fish held tight behind my knee —

tissue paper scarred from my bike skidding
on the gravel driveway, the fall
on my grandmother's sidewalk

and further up, a memory of your hands
on the one spot you like so much,
a place I never thought about before.

Furdale

There's a place where the river
bends low and wide, harbour of sky.

The geese will make their first vees
of the season from here, from your

slant of shoulders,
sweep of flashlight

mud sucking at our sneakers
under blankets of grass, waist-high.

When you brush poplars, whistle-soft
branches reach back and tangle my hair.

Your dog traces my steps in dark circles
as if I need herding, fences

or mending. Your slant
of shoulders, sweep
of flashlight.

saskatoon psalm

> be of love(a little) / More careful
> Than anything
> — e.e. cummings

watch how the mothers kiss their babies here,
careful on their cheeks

teach me to pronounce
sarcoma, dementia

clean a bathroom like it's sacred

love that you can't catch anything from sweat

teach me to wear gloves as if
this is the most fragile, more

gentle than breathing.

wreckoning

Vernal tick of hands,
twitches of time and face.

Sand slipping through, you listen
for the sea: cottonmouth whispers of salt
battened for storm weather, whelps
and shrieking tide.

No locks against the crackle
of air about to spark,
vicissitudes of rain.

Only hide-and-seek
with the sea.

The sky (cracking yolks over
clawed feet) says
grow thicker skin
for your boots
this winter.

❧ ❧ ❧

Spine, a string of
prayer wheels winding
a crow's nest in your hair.

The stars recalibrate.
Your knuckles swell,
spools of nerve and bone wound tight.

Steal yourself away,
leave a changeling
in your cradle:

garlic cloves for teeth,
a horseshoe smile.
Half-knit finger stitches,
clamshell toes.

Blanket your charms
with a woolen tongue.

Speak the tidings.

❧ ❧ ❧

Your house,
a curiosity shop of the sea:

windows lacy with brine,
curtained with sargassum.

Shelves of wave-worn glass,
the clock's familiar snowy face.

The roar of winter from the doorway
drowns your song.

Tread the ocean floor
on the tips of your fingers,
shed your sealskin.

Unfold yourself anew.

tabula rasa

across from you, watching
ink spiral out of your hands
into stars & vines across paper

stretched blank between us
this blush twining up my neck
some affectionate sunburn

or hint of something blossoming
where before, there was only white.

surrealust

dizzy with art, i notice you
reading — a journal of frida kahlo's

turning the pages so delicately
i wondered if you were afraid
to smudge the overripe blossoms
of colour

onto your fingers. and then
if you were to touch my face
again, or snatch my hand into yours

(charcoal under the nails
clipped short)

we'd both be a mess of secondhand colour,
red shawls, green hummingbirds
and bathtubs,

and maybe i'd feel
the way kahlo felt
about a woman
once.

Grey Area

It doesn't bother her so much, that grey area beneath her
    collarbone — just that it's not
grey, the way a pigeon isn't grey. More like an oilslick, shift-
    shining green and violet
over charcoal feather smears.

At night, her skin draws itself aside like curtains. She imagines
    the not-grey area
flickering its slick light across her bedroom wall, casting shadow-
    spells while she sleeps.

Her heart, sparrow's heart. Her lungs dowitcher wings, her bones
    hollow as a pigeon's,
so light she rises like a siskin feather, like bread, pink lung
    balloons into charcoal-smear sky.

She rises, leaves the grey area shimmering, an oilslick on her
    pillow.

Nightjar

There is a dizzy spell between our mouths and a storm
on second avenue. My hands tangled in yours and a two-step
waltz down an alley.

There are my sneakers skidding on dark, wet gravel
an empty bluestreak of sidewalk.

Your face turned skyward, slick with rain and streetlight,
a downpour of a girl.

A monsoon of honey inside me, your mouth dovetailing
into a smile, a tempest larkspurred in your eyes.

There is a shiver like storm window glass
and my laugh drowsy with shisha in the auricle of your ear.

Love poems from a bridge

I hadn't seen you for a month
and I was already drunk on something cold and glassy with limes.

You offered me a spoonful of the margarita
cradled in a thermos between your knees.

When the storm broke, you left. Went dancing in the rain.
Caught pneumonia, and I was smitten.

I made you promise to come back if the lights were on,
and I left the lights on all night.

I watched thunderbolts from an upstairs window,
sick on someone else's bed.

All the traffic lights flashed green at four a.m.
graffiti on the bridge.

It said, *if one night you were to die*
and your body decayed into a thousand stars,
could I be your sky?

mortuary

this river valley is silver-speaking in tongues

you will be sleeping beneath
slack-jawed blankets, the hiss
of gravel, and through spiderweb cracks
in your windshield

it will be whispering all the while

and you wake from a dream of nautical stars
or sea glass and remember how to find
cassiopeia, sagittarius or maybe just north
again.

and you will leave the flashlight
in the car, remember shearwater night
and borealis, prairie bear and sagebrush
diamond willow

you run your fingertips over the hills
and remember

this is how you spell
cretaceous
this is how you articulate
a spine

you wonder how
you ever forgot.

everything stops for the wind

what if love made me live here
on the land that made you?

it's how i get to know this highway, ditch lilies
and narrow shoulders

how i learn to tilt with the wind
that shaped your bones

unwraps teeth from whitemud jackets
on an oligocene hill

this wind that whickers down into coulees
kisses my eyes with dust
splinters a rearview mirror into sky-blue lace

this wind's got something to say.
when it pauses for breath,
everything in the valley stops:

crickets, monarchs, paints and sparrows,
frenchman river, sweetgrass sky holds still

out here, everything stops
for the wind.

Preservation

That summer you brought me bones:
thoracic vertebrae, garfish teeth.

Ash under your nails older than cypress,
red imprint of an incisor on your palm.

Sidestepping quicksand slow & homesick
you sent lunate blisters, corvid skulls
from the ravine at Hell Creek. Fossil valentines —

traces of inland sea so deep
you can sink your feet in
and feel saltwater in the dust,

craters of grass,
the shells of dead rivers.

Your entire collection, comparative.
Nothing I'll give you will last.

Who's to know

Tell me about her. It's Sunday morning at the Mandarin;
I'm running on three hours of sleep, jasmine tea, and coconut
rolls sticky between my fingers. Red and gold paper dragons snap
at the corners of my eyes, my hands unfolding fortune cookie
consolation sweet across my tongue. *Tell me a story.* Tail end of
April, sky the colour of a sunburned wrist—cloudy blue veins
beneath an orange peel of delicate skin. River a shady twist in
the prairie, no place for a snake-catching, steel-eyed girl. Her
bluebitten gaze following me through the grass long after I
look away. Yellowjackets, waxwings, cattails whisper their dry,
raincraving song. *Tell me everything.* Once I came this close to
a deer, I explained, the green in her eyes suspending insects in
the hearts of trees. Once I fell asleep in a shoal of blankets on
his floor, the boy with the shaved head and necklace of monk
skulls, his ear turned against my skin as if he was listening
for the ocean. He asked if I come here often, if I've done this
much before. This is why I wore shoes I could walk home alone
in. *Tell me what happened.* I woke up and said goodbye to the
houseplants, their shadows tangled across his face. Out in the
afterdark, the motion light stuttered as I passed by her place,
alone with a sharkcage in my chest and listening to the shiver
rise up from the trees by the river—stretching, leaves dark and
green-veined, collecting my thoughts. I know the graffiti on the
tailbones of these bridges like your tattoos, healing like braille
beneath my fingers. I know the last time I woke up, I forgot
my hands in a dream. I know the last time I needed a mirror,
you told me to look in your eyes. The last time, you recited
all the bones between us until I fell asleep. How do you name
these body parts I never knew I had so easily? When I wake up
carrying trust like a bowl of honey inside me, I want to smear
letters across the pavement for the sweet talking eyes of anyone

who wondered why I couldn't say yes. Because I was still looking in their mouths for a word. There isn't a word for us yet, but I can feel it heavy as a gold coin under my tongue, nasturtiumurmuring in my ear before I fall asleep. *Listen.* You'll be the first to know.

Catastrophe

Every girl I look at lately seems to have wings: freckled sparrow
    feathers
dusting a shoulder, tiny red doves behind her ear, a raven across
    her back.
I worry when you describe yourself as a cat.

Touch-me-nots

I fainted because my roommate potted fifty *mimosa pudica*
across our kitchen floor: bipinnate leaves,
syncope of elbows on ceramic.

Sensitive plants: brush the tips of their leaves and they collapse,
droop like high school — you'd touch me and I'd break out
in hives, wither. Some part of adaptation.

Draw a map for lover's hands in the dirt —
here, and not here.

Grow touch-me-nots,
shrinking violets.

Botanical tantrums,
how I close up so gently.

Build me a greenhouse.
Let's not do this in the kitchen
anymore.

January

We do stupid things to keep warm:
knit rosaries of poems; our hands turn blue with veins.

I am soaked with your eyes:
Bombay sapphire, empty Tanqueray green.

trespassing

today i am chain-link
you're hooking your fingers through
bones and through
ink

Spring Break-Up

After you leave, I walk in my sleep
for the first time since childhood.

Middle of the night, startled awake
to the humming of the fridge
in my grandmother's kitchen,
eleven stories above the river.

This was always your habit:
wandering between slow waves
of parasomnia, cycles of night terror
sleep spindles piercing your fingers.

Insomniacs love me, say there's something
soporific in my fever dreams.

How I always sleep through their leaving
somniloquies, frozen

the fear of walking barefoot
into minus forty.

Menagerie

i.

The summer you went away
I kept his number on our fridge,
the man with the Gila monster
in the basement, *just in case*
anything goes wrong

though emergencies, like us,
were *unlikely.*

ii.

You, who call me crying,
motherless barn kitten cradled
to your chest for its final purr.

Me, who forgot to thaw
the baby mice in their glass
of warm water, fed one frozen

to your cold-blooded corn snake,
then coaxed it slowly back
from hibernation.

iii.

Yours, the kind of father
who, when we find
the baby porcupine at the wood shed
howls, *i'm gonna kill*
that sunnuvabitch

yet won't shoot
his own cattle.

Mine, the kind
who never owned a gun.

iv.

Me, who sprang the crickets
into the laundry, filled our washer
with the sound of marsh echoes,

neglected the terrarium,
its tiny waterfall, until
your tree frogs croaked
and shrivelled.

v.

When you find the tegu on craigslist,
a lizard the size of a house cat
who, for lack of sunlight, has lost
all its bones to the tiny fragments
of rickets

you spend your paycheque to end
its suffering. Your friend
the unlicensed vet brings euthanol
to our kitchen table, and I leave
to watch autumn fall into our windows.

You keep the cold checkerboard of its mortis
for your collection of bones,
even though they are shattered.

I loved you so much
I would have bought you a freezer
to keep the body.

vi.

Me, who learned to check the geckos
for pregnancy, to feel the heat of eggs
beneath their scales.

Turned our house upside down
to find the runaway skink,
a blue squirm under the doormat.

vii.

I still look away
even when you pin
the jeweled edges of insects
into picture frames.

viii.

You, collecting the shattered and dead,
and me, who lived.

at least

on any given night
there will be at least

two of us, awake & haunting
the empty that was you.

at least
i will always
have company.

Decisions

I never know who else I'll run into grieving up here, on the hill
    where your old lovers go,
the graveyard of pioneer children under the trees, and Grace
    Fletcher's headstone
at rest on her pile of bison bones.

Tonight there's a couple on a motorbike by the train bridge,
    setting off fireworks
with a cigarette, sounding gunshots into the thunderheads over
    the river.

If I have to be without you, I can't decide if I'll be the cigarette,
    the train bridge,
or the fireworks.

Unsent, No. 1

So I ran into your best friend in the alley behind the gay bar.
Tried to light her cigarette for her.
Seemed like the kind of thing you would have done.

It was too windy. We stood in the dark, hands cupped
over our faces, whispered just loud enough
for queens and clouds of smoke to hear us:

I'm ok, really, no
really,
ok.

Yartzeit

Or, the year of grief I have spent callusing
my hands to write a memory
for your father.

Like Scheherazade, he's asked me for a story
to keep away nightmares and needles,
your grandmother's anger,
your mooshum's shaking,
and the solitude of your mother.

It has been a year, and now
that my nails have grown back
from their bitten shreds,

now that I have pulled myself
from the kitchen floor,

now that the doorbell of your wake
has finally stopped ringing,

I am to write.

How do I tell your father
everything has already been written?

I loved my friend.
He went away from me.
That's all there is to say.

I could tell about our trip to the zoo
in high school, how the peacocks screamed
from the top of their hutch with tails fanned

how we chased chickens and stalked a wolf
with mange, talked burrowing owls

and the way the geese rushed at you,
hissed at our laughter.

These are the stories I can tell safely,

when we are ten or eleven, perched on the edge
of our seats in a dark theatre three hours north,
not knowing we are to grow up fifteen minutes away
from each other

in towns too small
to name ourselves

we are watching the same screen with wonder,
our faces upturned in the blue light, glowing
as if something tells us

you are going to love each other, someday.

And yet even after a year I'm bereft
of our late-night heresies.

Do I leave to your father's memory
how we sat in stained-glass light
on the steps of a church,

and you told me about the bathhouse,
the hotel rooms?

I want to keep that part of you.
Every small painful thing.

The third-degree burn on your hand
from the deep fryer.

The last time I saw you
and you told me I was beautiful.

To my lovers I bequeath the rest of my life
I want nothing left of me for you

Death, you have written everything already.
That's all there is to say.

I leave for your father a poem,
a woman who is talking to death, and a howl,
for *the best mind of my generation destroyed by madness,*

every small painful thing,
our faces upturned in the light.

Kaddish

You, my atheist, lover
of logic, absurdity

would laugh to hear me
mourn you in a Kaddish.

I would like to hear you laugh again —

Yit'gadal v'yit-kadash sh'may raba
Blessed is he, beyond any blessing
and song, praise and consolation
uttered in the world,
ve'imru amen.

Dry Spell

There's some fragile storm stirring between us:

my bones unraveled from their red sleeves,
hollowed with splinters of lightning,

a lacy matrix where veins
and common sense used to flicker.

Now when I comb my hair
I worry about brushfires —

ilium and ischium ablaze,
incendiary trillium of kindling.

The tips of my fingers matchsticks.
When you touch my hands, smoke.

She Was Right

Well, there was this one time, opening night of my first
show — I'm in the bathtub, heels tearing fishnet on the faucet,
this liquid silver junk on my lashes (it's like rails for your
eyes), orange juice and vodka sweet across my tongue tied
shy — madam's all done up

like Vegas molting pink feathers on the tile while she nukes
my head with hairspray and hot irons, and she's like, *are you a*
lesbian? and *what year of college are you in?*

and I'm feverish blushing like *no, and first* and she just kind of
smiles, and checks her lipstick in the mirror, grins and tells me
you've got time.

Meat Market

Late shift at the call centre —
in between hang-ups, he asks me
about moonlighting, my later job
as dancer:

Does your boyfriend mind
other men looking at you
like you're a piece of meat?

He is thinking: red lipstick
and tits on ice. Snow White
under glass. Something to sink
his teeth into.

Not meat, I tell him.
If everyone looked at me and saw
blood guts and muscle,
I'd never make any tips.

My girlfriend will butcher him later.

Never Have I Ever

I'm the girl who always drinks in this game, except with you.

Never chewed glass to growl, lit a car on fire, hitchhiked.

Your heart is an alarm set to wake me. When I rest
my head on your chest I hear it ticking.

When you tell me to steal something, I'll say

You go first.
Pick me.

Sugar

In the diner on 20th she teaches me
that icing sugar is an explosive:
So when I say we're baking a cake next weekend,
I really mean
my kitchen cupboards are full of arson.
I mean the taste of your mouth
makes my teeth ache.
I mean I delivered two dozen vegan explosives to your door
on your birthday.
I mean they won't let me on the plane
once you kiss me goodbye;
I've got a belly full of sugar powder
and your mouth on mine leaves a spark.

riot lung

in brooklyn i want your grit
on my face, your subway in my bones
to rattle and cement an ache under my feet,
the city grown over me in streets that shimmer
with catcalls and clouds of heat hanging from my collar

new york listens, gives me space, leaves me underground
with a memory of your hands where we are finally
in the same time zone and changing between phone calls

you're in toronto where they have seized
all the garbage bins as potential weapons
and the cops are using plastic bullets this year

i think of you every time they search my bag on the subway,
at the post office, at the library, at the african burial ground
the museum of jewish heritage at the UN at manhattan city hall
i think of you when they search my bag at pride

and afterwards when you call me, i'm the girl on the sidewalk
with a loud voice and her heart in her hand like a seashell
instead of a cell phone, when you call me

i'm just outside of ground zero at night, it's a construction site
lit up with spotlights, a gap in the skyline like a tooth,
like a heart murmur, like the delay between
your *can you hear me* and my *yes*

the reception out here is patchy and i'm trying
to hold on to your voice between static, your voice
deeper after a month of speaking french
you sound deeper and ocean salt and steady when you tell me

i really can't afford to go to jail right now
but if i'm not arrested by saturday
i'm doing something wrong.

i don't know how to tell you i think
you're doing everything right

so i watch every news clip twice looking for your face
i think of you every time i set off a metal detector
at ellis island, at the statue of liberty
at laguardia and at pearson

i think of you on canada day
when for the past five years on this night
i would go down to the river for the fireworks
to watch them spark red above the trees.

this year, there are no fireworks for me
after your stories of vinegar and burning

no fireworks for a country
with this much tear gas

a country i left with a backpack,
the notebook you gave me, enough
money to get home and pay your bail
if you needed it

a country where i get through customs
with a smile on my face
and a four-chambered hand grenade
in the left side of my ribcage

a country where if you need it
i'll always come back

Righteous

You make me want
    to paint my nails red
    to match my dress
    to your best friend's boots
    for the rockabilly show at Walker's.

Collar turned up, how you
    danced me in circles
    cradled a beer in the small of my back.

How the jerk
    with the blue mohawk slammed hard into me twice, how you
    watched me plant both hands against his chest.

You said I *schooled* him.
    Smiled when I blushed, prideful.

You're the first to call me
    fierce, righteous.

Corner of Broadway & 11th, the first
    person to ever kiss me
    in broad daylight.

The Visit

It is never too rainy for protestors.

I had spent too long turning students away at a checkpoint
on the wrong side of the fence. The safe side. Too long in
the rain in heels and a dress; I don't even know how to dress
conservatively.

Every single car in his motorcade splashed me on the way by.

Could you imagine how much trouble we would have gotten into
with that cop's raincoat?

How the security dyke wouldn't stop staring. My unspoken
request: at least ask me to marry you, and see what your boss
has to say about it.

He's the man who built cages out of Queen Street,
sent his riot scarabs after you, wings clicking.

Panic made me gnaw my knuckles,
ask for the watch list from the guard:

unfolding,
the one time I dreaded
to see your face.

little metaphors for criminals

i.

at your house i've got a paper cut:
looking for band-aids,
all i can find
is a rifle.

ii.

don't tell me i was a shotgun
blast through your heart,

i left because you were
thinking about guns.

If I Had To

I could pick your hands out of a prison line-up if I had to.
(Please let me never have to.)

Two broken fingers, tiny white scar on your palm
sun rash of tattoo on your inner arm.

I wonder if you've still got a picture of me
in your wallet to show *the other guys.*
(Please let you never have to.)

I still get heart attacks for denim jackets,
every ginger urchin with a septum ring
is you.

I'd still keep my promises, please
let me never have to.

Reasons

(for Calondra)

Because when I visit you at Wreck Beach,
salt dreadlocked in your hair and honey in your eyes
I hate to think of you curled like a snailshell at the edge of this
    ocean city
alone or worse in a reef of coastal light, your voice like whiskey-
    cherries lost in sleep.
Because the air is grey and sour
and because you still smell like cinnamon and olive oil.
Because I like to think the prairie and its razorbilled horizon
    miss you too.
And there will be lilacs soon. Come home.

Night Shift

I look for you between ECGs and nearly miss
your silhouette in sliding doors of light.

Hours ago, we lay shirtless in my backyard
with beer and sweated into sun-withered grass.

Nights have shifted you into a shadow
of scrubs and silver stethoscope necklace.

The buzzer at your hip gives me shivers. Already illicit,
my handfuls of coffee brought to you at the old hospital entrance.

Now somewhere, someone is having a heart attack
while we burn our tongues in the dark and whisper.

But you laugh. *If it was important, they would have said stat.*
If they don't need a heart tracing, that person probably didn't make it.

I don't really understand your job.
I think I would like a heart tracing.

Tomorrow morning, you will collapse into sleep, your night
fibrillated with contact precautions.

I sleep with my phone on in case of emergencies.
When your text sirens me awake at one a.m. coastal time

it could only be three things: a slow night (no cardiac arrests
at home) and maybe you're thinking of me.

this is the sound

(for Alison)

this is the sound the good ink makes,
the way soaked paper will sink
up to your wrists in pulp and sizing,
the methyl heat between your fingers.

here we find our rhythm of
ghostprint, wash hands,
swill coffee.

i have always been a mess
of inkfingers and bruises,
the girl with her own thumbs
for thimbles. i don't remember
the last time i wore an apron.

now you teach me
how to turn the ship's wheel
of a press, tighten until it kicks back,
blot rags and newspaper.

you point out the box
of rosin marked "cancer."
i think, everything in this room
could kill me. you assure
that it would only be slowly.

i have forgotten how little
i trust my own hands, but
i can learn.

this is the sound
the good ink makes.

Blood Oranges

she in   spires   me

and my breath, a night breeze rustling dark where something like
an orange grows trestled sleek and tight between bronchi branch,
lung and lullaby of anastole, diastole,
heart   you   stole
and my whole   body stings like a cracked mouth
kissing a persimmon, fingertips stained
red   sore   sour
something like an orange midsummer moon-heavy horizon
splitting into crescents trailing fragile wet ghazals
across   my   ribs
humming with sushumna singing salamandarin tangerine
you incarnadine my green. you sibylline my serpentine
sink   your   teeth
into this sistine apple slow, tonguing
oolong   orchard   chai   let it grow
loon   song   sigh